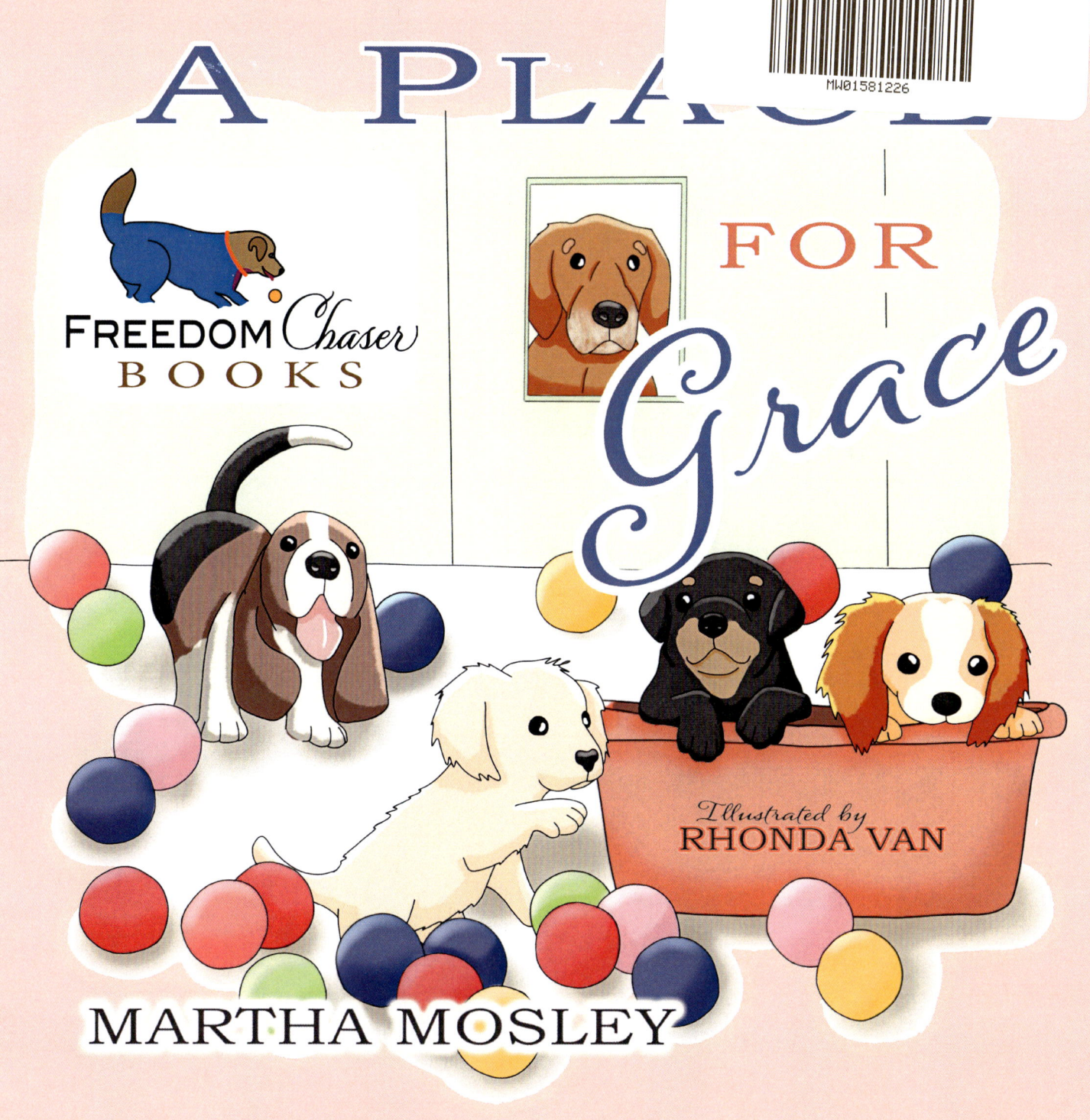

Copyright 2022 by Martha Mosley
All rights reserved.

No part of this book may be reproduced in any form or by electronic means, including information storage and retrieval systems, without written permission from the publisher, except by a reviewer, who may quote passages in a review.

Published by FreedomChaser Books
an imprint of Who Chains You Publishing
FreedomChaserBooks.com · WhoChainsYou.com

Written by Martha Mosley

Illustrated by Rhonda Van
rhondaluluart.com

Cover and Interior design by Tamira Thayne
tamirathayne.com

Paperback ISBN: 978-1-954039-23-0

Printed in the United States of America

First Edition

Dedication

Thanks to Danielle and Myrlene.
What would I have done without you?

Grace must be invisible.

She can see her two front paws
and her furry red chest.

If she spins fast enough, she can
even see the white tip of her tail.

She thinks others can't see her, though.

Why else would they hurry past
without saying hello?

She doesn't like this
scary place called a "shelter."

It has cold, hard floors,
and is noisy, even at night.

They say that dogs here have no homes.

Grace always had a home.

When she was a puppy,
she went to live with the Millers.

When Chris threw balls, Grace chased them.

When Kate played music, Grace sang along.

They said she was their perfect dog.

Grace knows some things
had changed as time passed.

The children grew up and moved away.

When he came to visit, Chris didn't
have time to throw balls.

When Grace sang,
Kate said, "Be quiet."

Then Mr. and Mrs. Miller
said they wanted a smaller house.

Any place was fine with Grace
as long as she was with them.

A sign at the new place changed
everything, though. It said:
NO DOGS ALLOWED

That was when they brought her here.

Grace cried when they left her.

She waited for them to come back.
They did not come.

Now Grace watches puppies
leave to go to new homes.

"We want a young dog," people say.

Grace is not a young dog,
but she needs a home too.
She has to make someone want her.

She will show that she
is playful like a puppy.

She jumps high in the air.

She falls down hard and bumps her tail.

That didn't work.

She will look cute like a puppy.

She holds her head high and blinks her eyes.

"That dog looks silly," someone says.

That didn't work.

She will be friendly like a puppy.

She pulls her lips back in her biggest smile.

"That dog wants to bite us," a lady says.

No one understands...

"Our family needs a really good dog."

Grace's heart thumps.
They are looking at HER!

They don't care that her face is gray.
Her eyes are wise and kind.

They don't care that she can't chase balls.
She can still play.

They don't care that
her voice wobbles.

She sings sweet songs.

"Grace, you won't chew our shoes,
pee on our floor, or wake us at night.
You already know how to live in a family.
Let's go home."

Grace's heart explodes with joy!

She spins circles in the air.

She sings the highest notes
she's ever sung.

Her new family understands!

Love never grows old.

Grace is their perfect dog.

The End

Why Adopt an Older Dog?

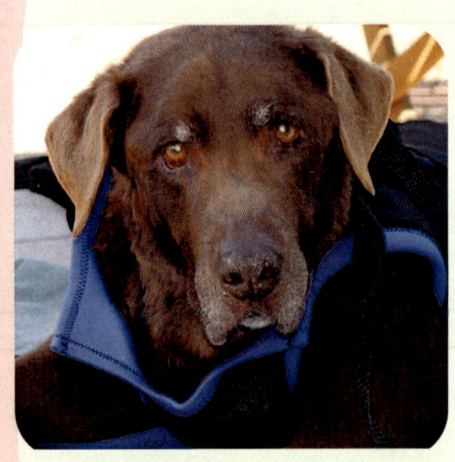

One word I often use to describe creating **Marty's Place Senior Dog Sanctuary** is "journey." It's been an interesting one, with twists and turns, but also many rewarding moments. Because of our own experience with a dog named Marty, we set out to help the neediest dogs—older dogs that face an uncertain future when they don't have a home.

Why consider welcoming an older dog into your home? It takes much longer for a senior dog in a shelter to find a home, and many are overlooked. With an older dog, you'll know what you are getting with regard to their size, health, and behavior. They generally know basic commands, still have the ability to learn, and form very special relationships.

If you would like to add a dog to your family, be clear about what you're looking for in a new companion—a running buddy, or one who lies with you on the sofa. Small, large, quiet, or playful, older dogs can fit your lifestyle and be a great match!

It warms our hearts whenever we place one of our residents in an adoptive or forever foster home. Another dog like Grace is out there waiting and available to give you the same opportunity for love!—**Doreen Jakubcak, Marty's Place Senior Dog Sanctuary, martysplace.org**

Love Never Grows Old!

Testimonials from Adopters of Older Dogs

DAISY DUKE. "We had the honor of adopting Daisy Duke, an 8-year-old coonhound. Daisy loved all eight of our grandchildren and helped Faith, our shy Golden Retriever understand what it means to be a dog. Though Daisy was always grateful to us, we were the ones who were blessed."—*Pat Robertson, Secretary, Ocean County Volunteer Auxiliary for Animal Shelters*

PIG. "Though our rescue usually takes pregnant moms or puppies, we made an exception and adopted a 7-year-old stray named Pig. She became the rescue's mascot, comforting new dogs and welcoming adopters. She traveled with us from coast to coast, loved kids and other dogs, and made us forever grateful for her presence." —*Starrmarie Barry, President, All 4 The Dogs Rescue*

CINNAMON. "At age seven, Cinnamon was on death row in a Los Angeles shelter, thought to be too old and scarred for adoption—our last minute rescue mission saved her. She was a guardian, protector, cuddly goofball, and best friend who brightened the lives of everyone lucky enough to meet her."—*Joanne Conte Carr, Helping 4 Paws at a Time Pet Food Pantry*

ELLA. "Adopters sometimes say two or three year old dogs are 'too old.' We find that 4-year-olds like Ella do well in our service dog program because they are mature enough to learn easily and still have long lives ahead."—*Kelly Greschak, Founder, Jonah's Ark Animal Rescue*

DUALLY. "In my 15 years of training dogs, I've learned that desire to learn, not age, is what matters. It makes me smile to see white-faced seniors parading around, proud of new skills. The idea that old dogs can't be taught new things is simply not true."—*Elizabeth Casterlin Owner, Trainer J&R Kennels*

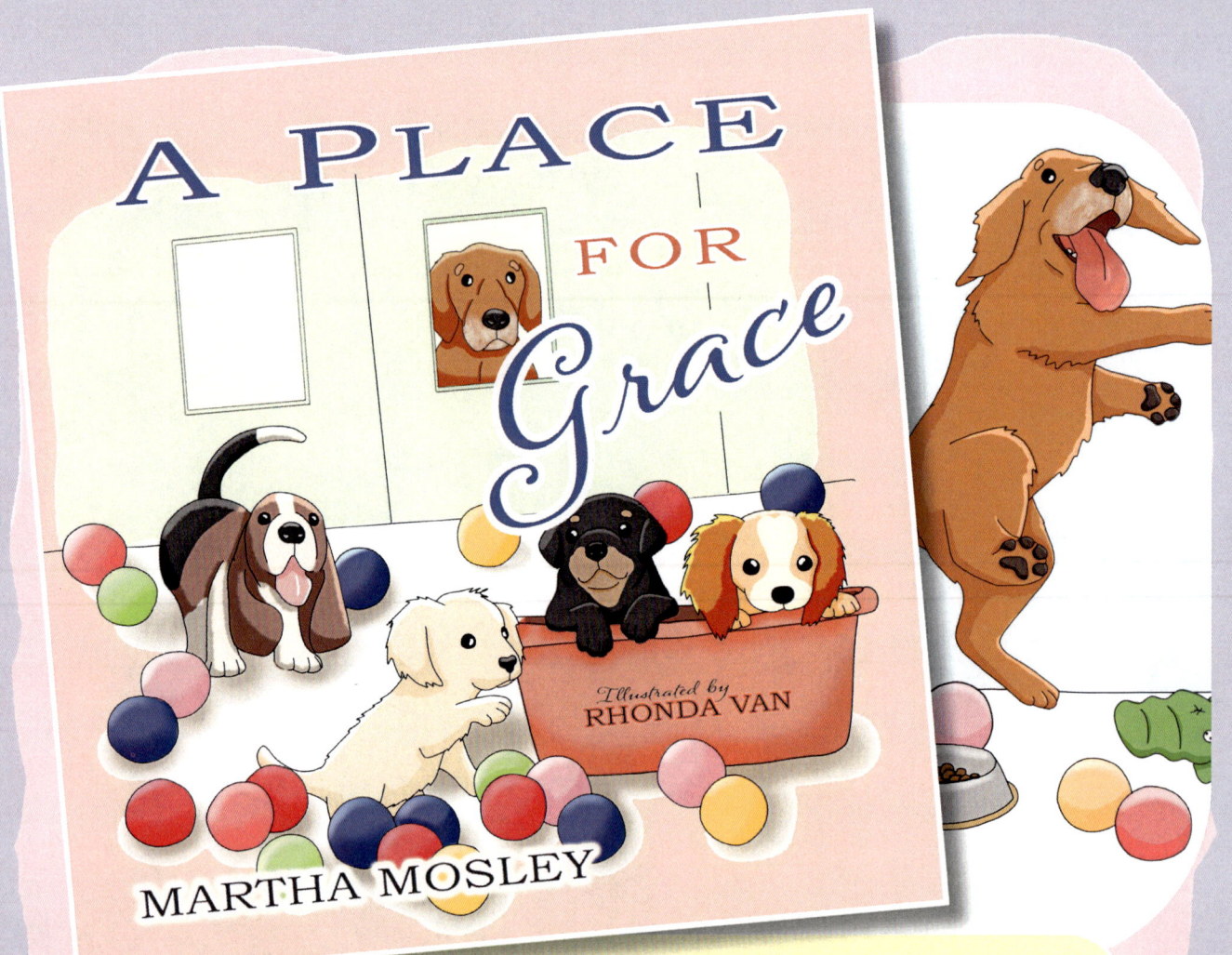

Love the book? Please consider giving *A Place for Grace* a review on your venue of purchase. Your reviews mean the world to our authors. *Thank you!*

About the Author

First time author **Martha Mosley** brings her love and respect for senior dogs to this story of an older dog in need of a new start. A believer in the value of the seasoned love that older dogs offer, Martha has spent a lifetime supporting rescue through fundraising and volunteerism.

When not working as an R.N., Martha spends her time reading, swimming, and gardening. She lives in New Jersey with her husband Howard, her daughter Michelle, and their three dogs: Happy and GiGi, both age 8, and Remy Martin, age 16.

About the Illustrator

Rhonda Van is an artist, author, wildlife rehabber, and life-long animal lover.

She particularly adores jackrabbits, squirrels, her animal companions, Shark Week, vegan dinners in Santa Cruz, and her husband Tony.

Rhonda has been drawing forever, but only got deeper into illustration after she started drawing the wildlife friends she cares for.

Rhonda is the author and illustrator of *Squeak the Squirrel*, and the illustrator of *A Place for Grace, Pal the Pig, The Big Wind, The No Name Bunny, The Sleepy Honey Bee, Lop-Eared Lily, Spittin' Kitten's Speed-Away,* and *Tiffany Rolls On.* Find her online at rhondaluluart.com.

About FreedomChaser Books

At FreedomChaser, we publish books for those who believe people—and animals—deserve to be free

We bring you books that educate, entertain, and share gripping plights of the animals we serve and those who rescue and stand in their stead.

We offer all kinds of stories about all kinds of animals: dogs, cats, rats, cows, pigeons, horses, pigs, snails, squirrels, birds, chickens, and many more! *Visit our site and read more about us at freedomchaserbooks.com.*

Also for Dog Lovers from FCB

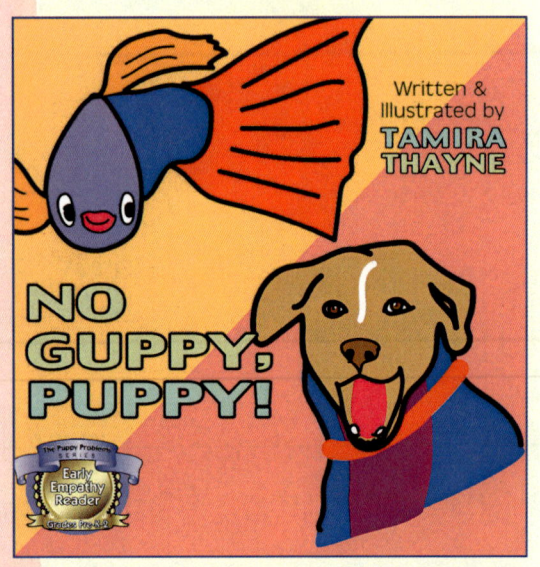

No Guppy, Puppy! introduces our littlest readers to lots of new animal friends as we learn about Puppy's little problem: he likes to chase animals!

But guess what? The other animals don't want to be chased. So Mom gives Puppy something fun and safe to do for each animal they meet.

In the end, Puppy finally sees someone Mom will let him chase…shhh…you'll have to read the story to find out who it is!

Written and illustrated by Tamira Thayne, **No Guppy, Puppy!** seeks to introduce young readers ages 3 and up to both early sight words and the animals we can see on our daily walks. Find it online at freedomchaserbooks.com.

Also for Dog Lovers from FCB

Cassius, an 8-year-old pitbull, has been stuck in the shelter for quite some time. It becomes his mission to rally all the other "special needs" animals together to change adopters' minds and find loving homes for himself and his friends.

This time, the Paws 'n Claws Adoption Day turns into a life lesson for all. Cassius keeps his friends positive and their heads held high, proving that looking different is not a bad thing—in fact, being yourself is the best way to be.

Different is Beautiful is a heart-warming story for children ages 7 and up that helps them accept people who may not look the same as they do. Find it at freedomchaserbooks.com.

Other Titles from

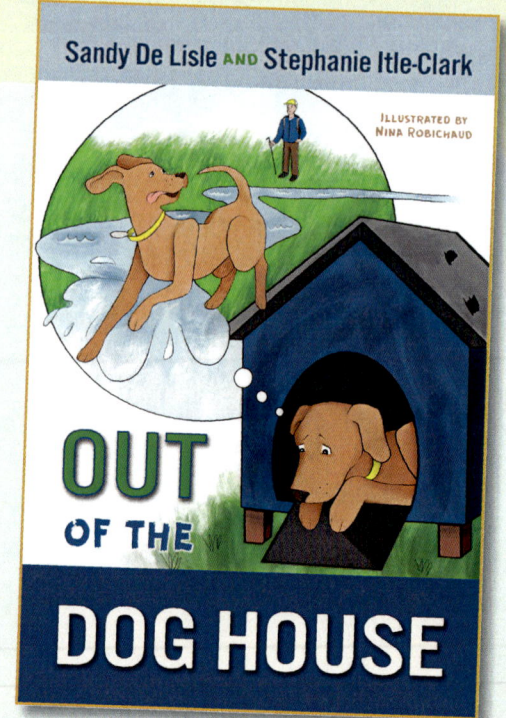

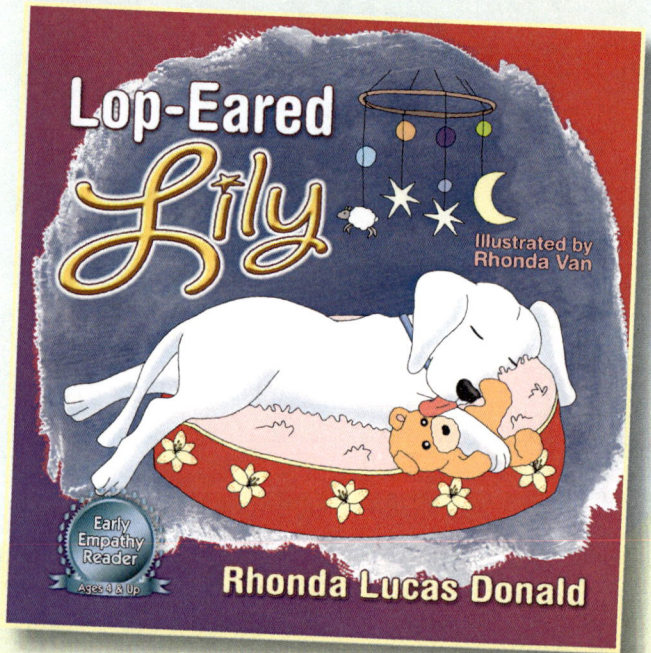

Freedomchaserbooks.com

Made in United States
North Haven, CT
11 December 2022